ONE HUNDRED words

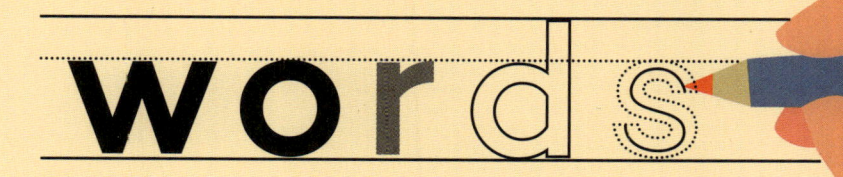

Anna Kövecses

WIDE EYED EDITIONS

HOW TO HOLD YOUR PENCIL

1 Use your thumb and your index finger to gently pinch the pencil.

2 Flip the pencil so that it is resting against the base of your index finger.

3 Use your middle finger to support the pencil from underneath. Now you have mastered the "tripod grip"!

Some tips and tricks:

a If you find yourself wanting to use more fingers for extra support, try holding a ball of cotton wool against your palm with your fourth and fifth fingers as you write (holding the pencil with your thumb, index and middle fingers).

b Use a shorter pencil – this means you will have less space to cram unnecessary fingers onto the pencil.

c Try using a pencil grip to help you with this new challenge.

THE TRIPOD GRIP

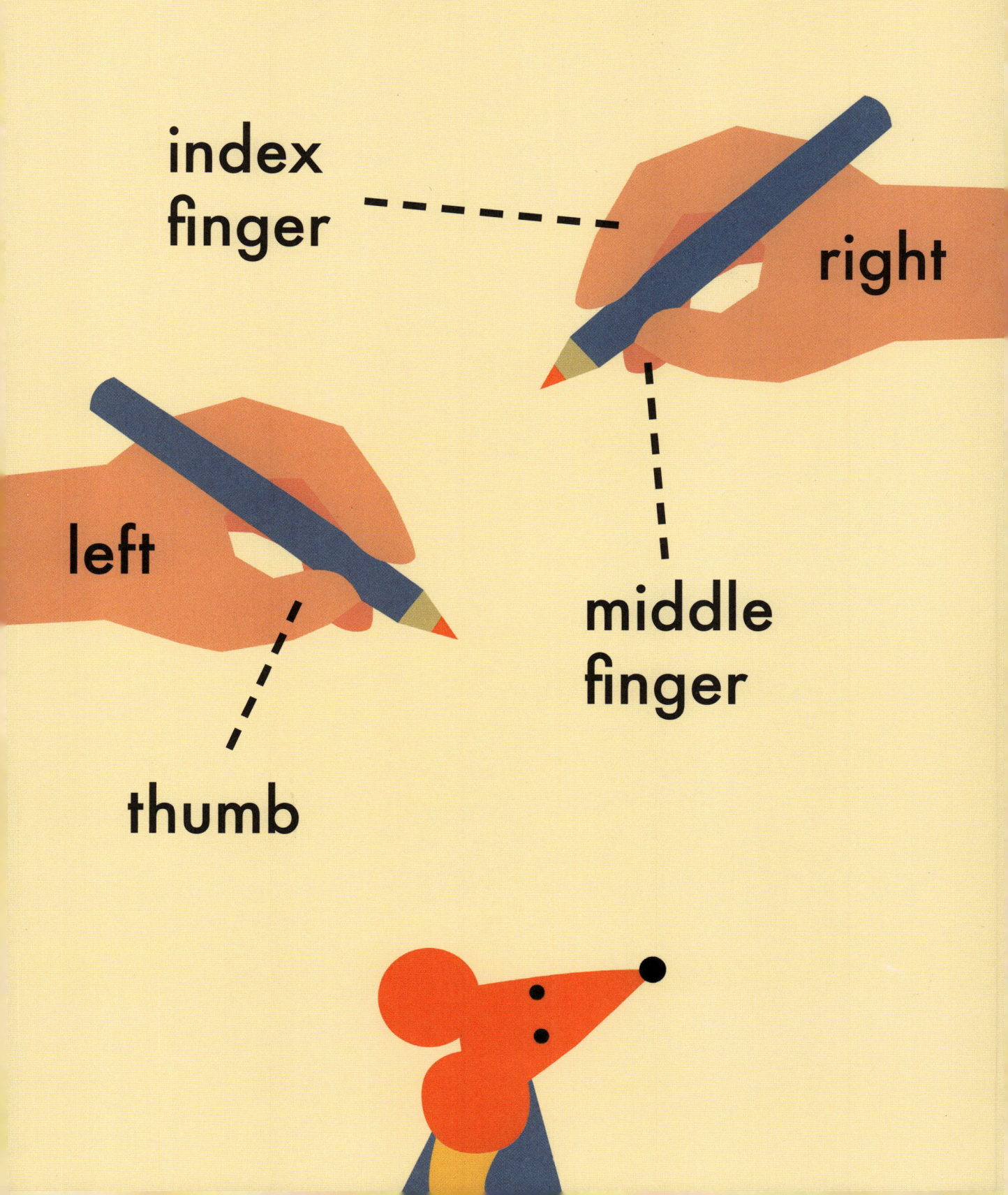

index finger

right

left

middle finger

thumb

CAN YOU DRAW A STRAIGHT LINE FROM SIDE TO SIDE?

Trace

CAN YOU DRAW A STRAIGHT LINE FROM TOP TO BOTTOM?

Trace

CAN YOU DRAW A DOWNWARD DIAGONAL LINE?

CAN YOU DRAW AN UPWARD DIAGONAL LINE?

CAN YOU DRAW A LOOPED LINE?

CAN YOU DRAW A CURVED LINE?

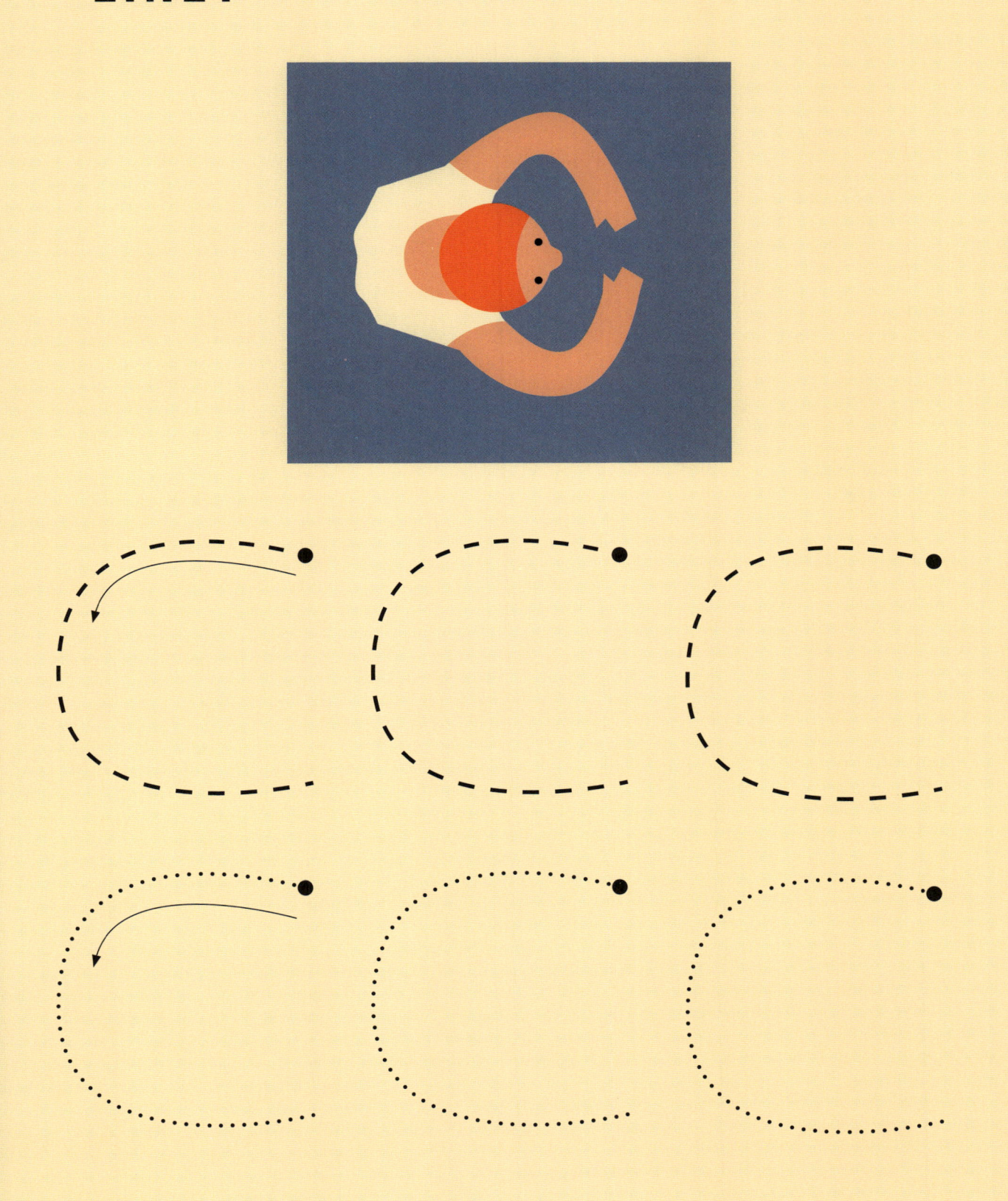

CAN YOU DRAW A ZIGZAG LINE?

CAN YOU DRAW A WAVY LINE?

CAN YOU DRAW A CIRCLE?

CAN YOU DRAW A SQUARE?

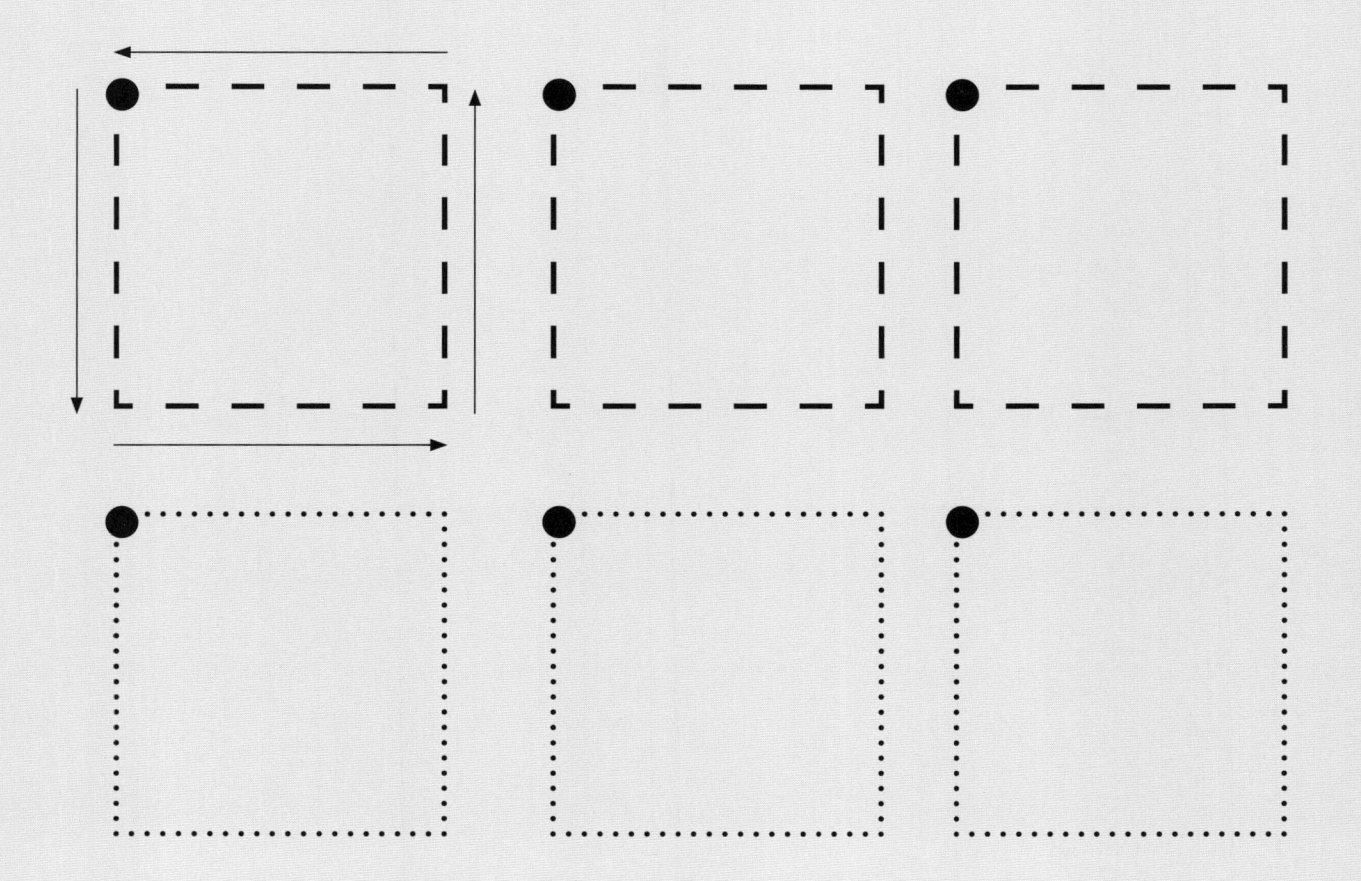

CAN YOU DRAW A STRAIGHT-EDGED SHAPE?

CAN YOU DRAW A CURVED SHAPE?

CAN YOU COPY ALL THE LETTERS OF THE ALPHABET?

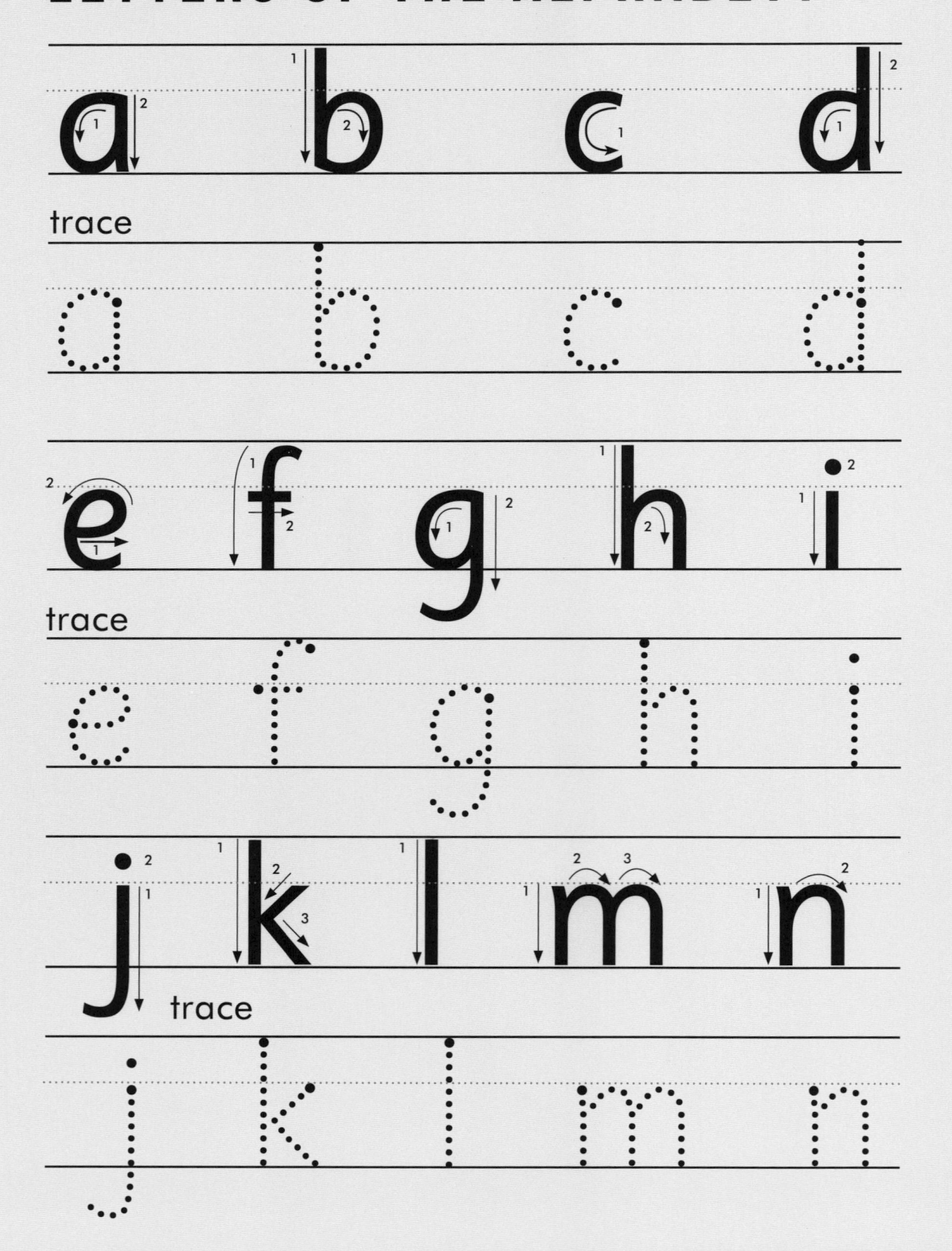

a b c d

trace

a b c d

e f g h i

trace

e f g h i

j k l m n

trace

j k l m n

o p q r

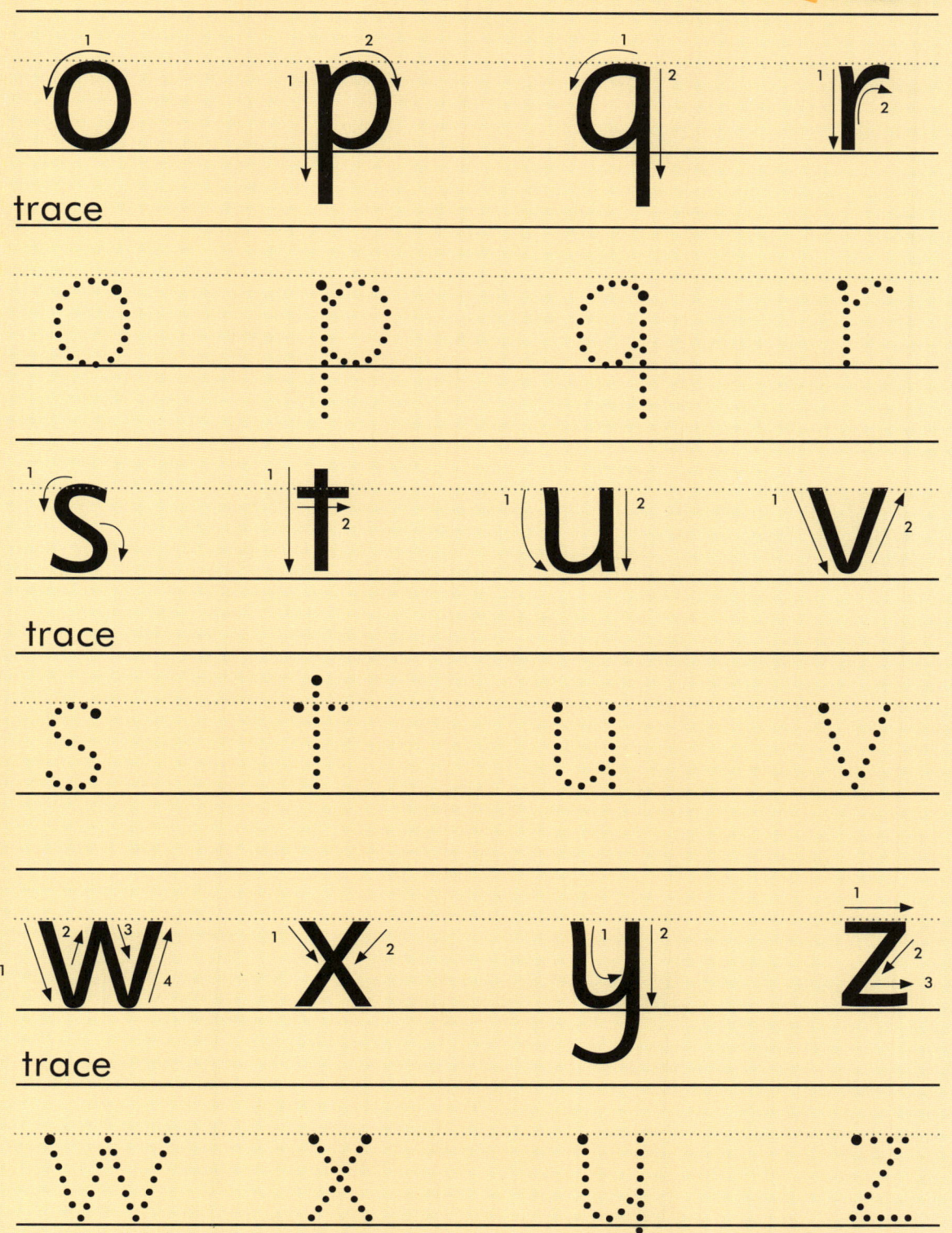

trace

o p q r

s t u v

trace

s t u v

w x y z

trace

w x y z

CAN YOU WRITE YOUR FIRST LETTERS?

a a a

b b b

c c c

d d d

e e e

f f f

g g g

h h h

i i i

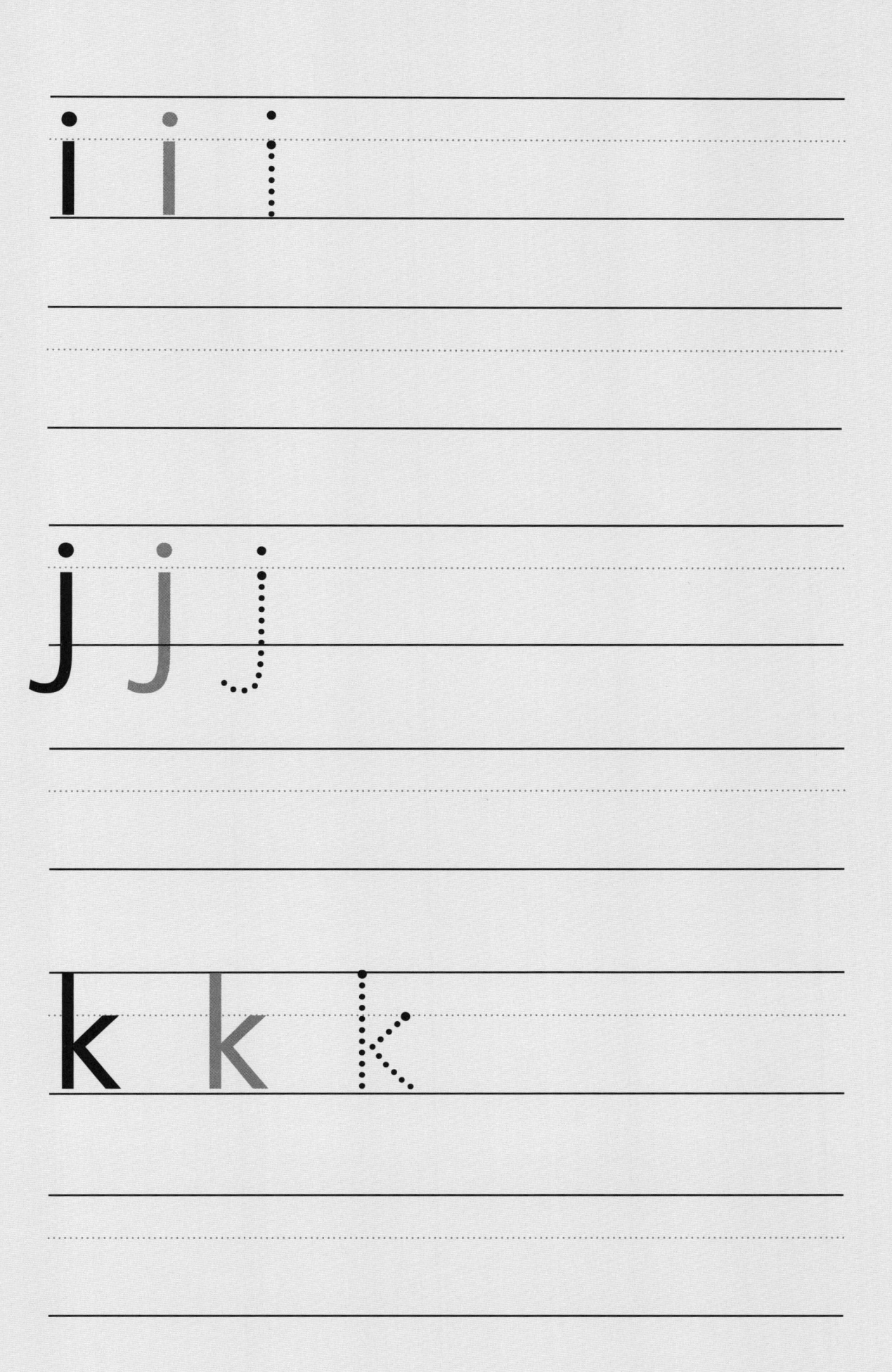

j j j

k k k

l l l

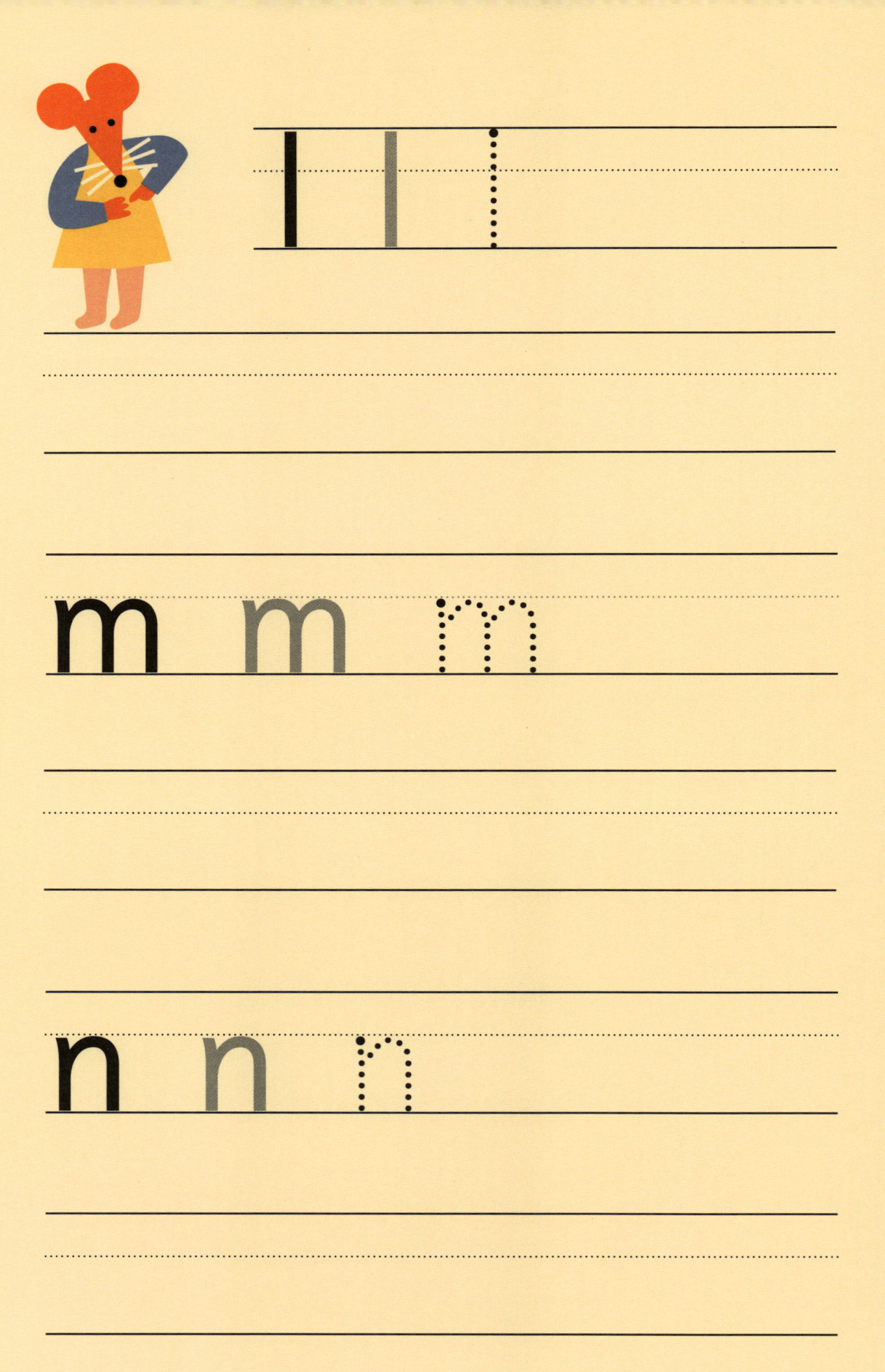

m m m

n n n

o o o

p p p

q q q

r r r

s s s

t t t

u u u

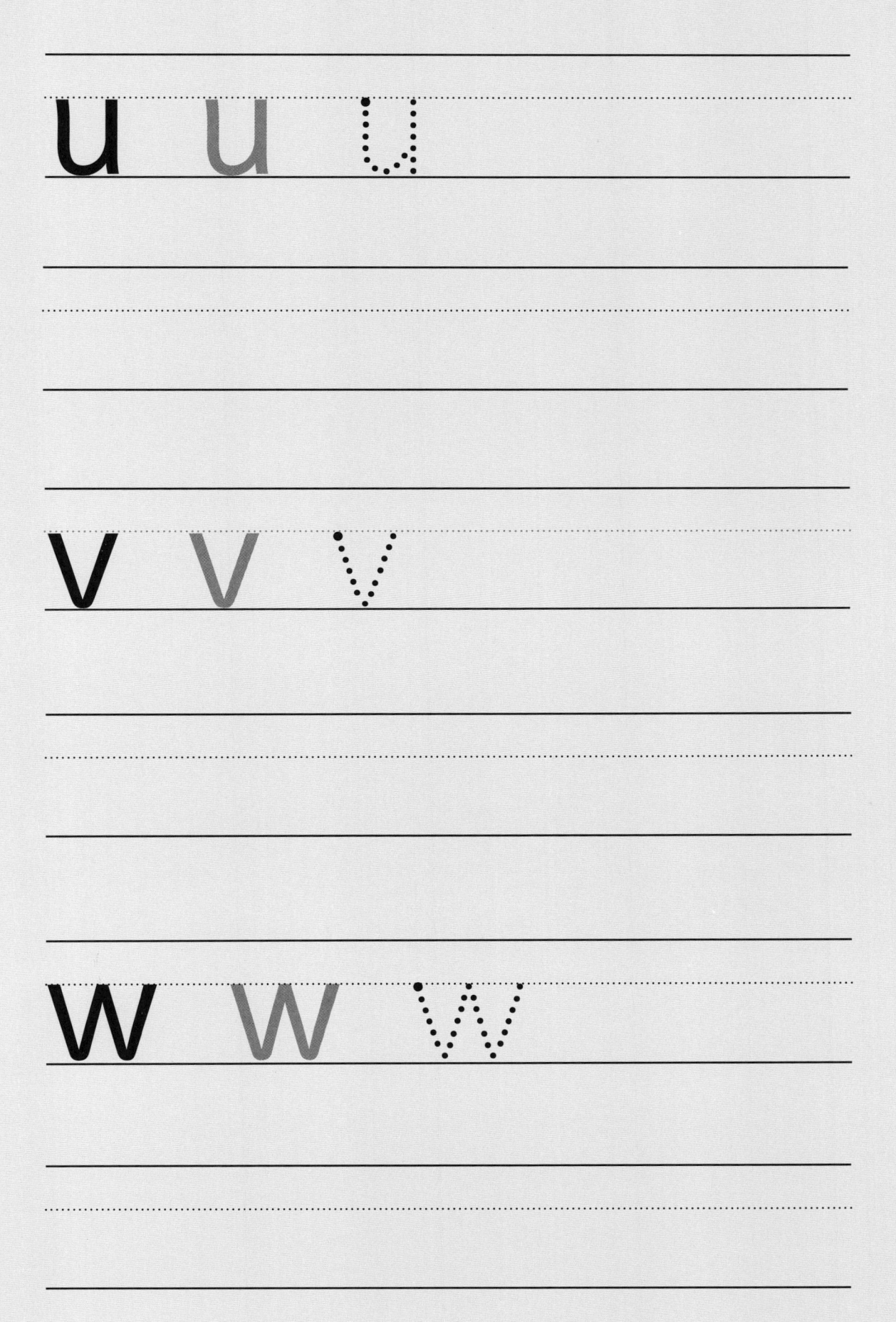

v v v

w w w

x x x

y y y

z z z

NOW CAN YOU WRITE A SENTENCE THAT USES ALL THE LETTERS OF THE ALPHABET?

the quick

brown fox

jumps over

the lazy

dog

CAN YOU ADD THE FIRST LETTERS?

pig

all

ractor

og

rab

gg

love

at

CAN YOU ADD THE MIDDLE LETTERS?

ban_a_na

l _ k

s _ ck

s _ n

ball_ _n

p_n

f_sh

dr_ss

CAN YOU ADD THE LAST LETTERS?

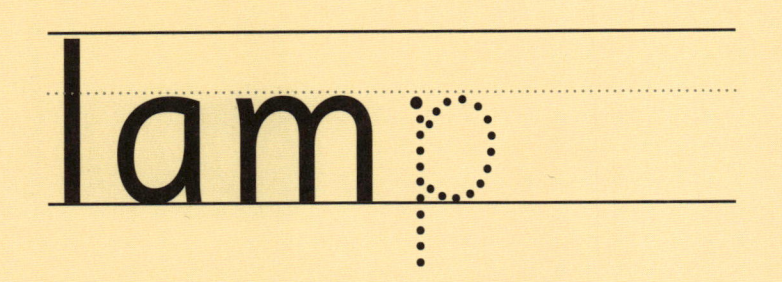

lamp

fla

tomat

cloc

bir

bea

shir

pea

CAN YOU SPELL YOUR NUMBERS FROM ONE TO FIVE?

1 one

2 two

3 three

4 four

5 five

one

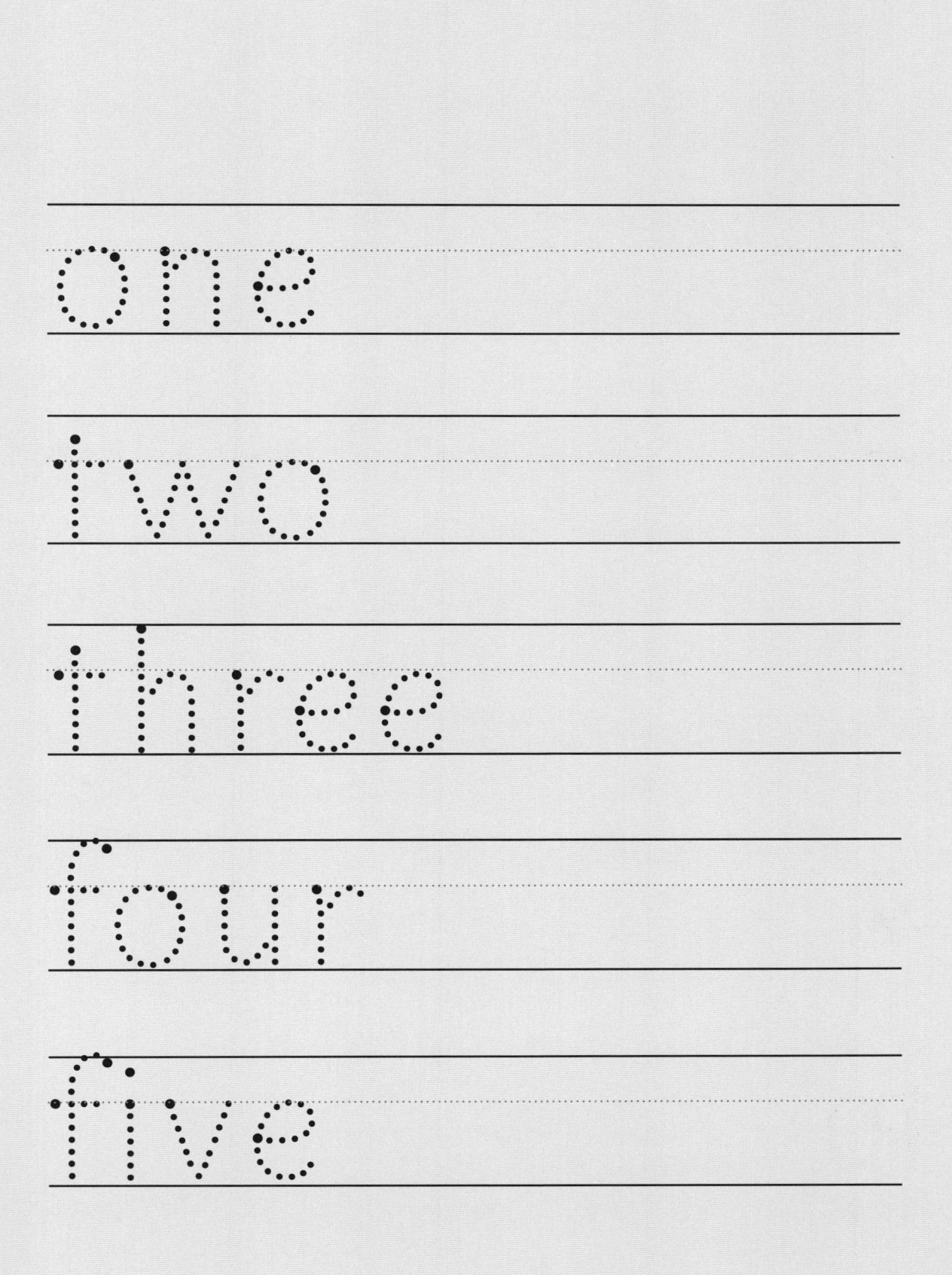

two

three

four

five

CAN YOU SPELL YOUR NUMBERS FROM SIX TO TEN?

6 six

7 seven

8 eight

9 nine

10 ten

six

seven

eight

nine

ten

CAN YOU WRITE YOUR NUMBERS FROM ONE TO TEN?

0   1   2

0   1   2

3   4   5

3   4   5

6 7 8

6 7 8

9 10

9 10

CAN YOU COUNT THE NUMBER OF THINGS?

How many tools are there?

_____

How many books are there?

_____

How many trees are there?

_____

How many leaves are there?
_____
_____

How many raindrops are there?
_____
_____

How many pips are there?
_____
_____

CAN YOU WRITE YOUR COLOURS?

red

yellow

blue

green

WHAT COLOURS ARE THESE THINGS?

CAN YOU WRITE YOUR COLOURS?

purple

orange

brown

pink

WHAT COLOURS ARE THESE THINGS?

_____
_____
_____

_____
_____
_____

_____
_____
_____

_____
_____
_____

CAN YOU WRITE THE NAMES OF THESE THINGS YOU CAN EAT?

orange

cherry

peach

apple

chilli

garlic

onion

cabbage

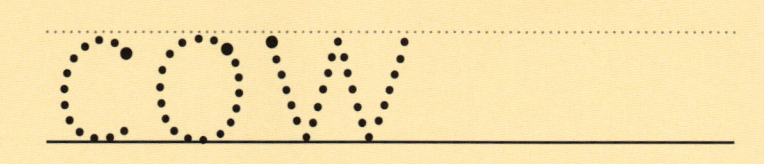

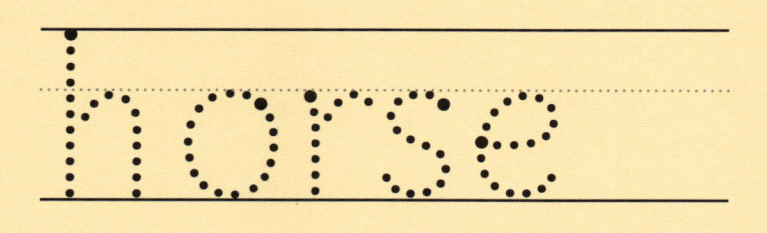

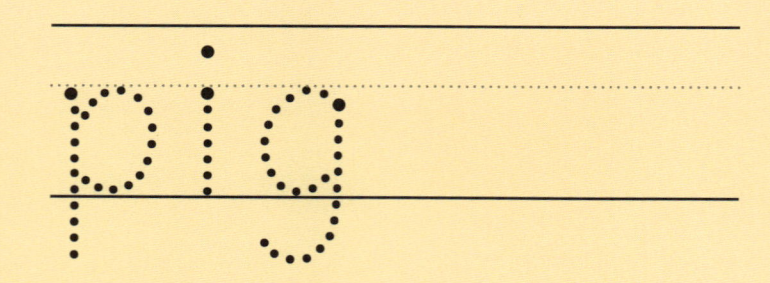

CAN YOU WRITE THE NAMES OF THESE ANIMALS?

cow

horse

pig

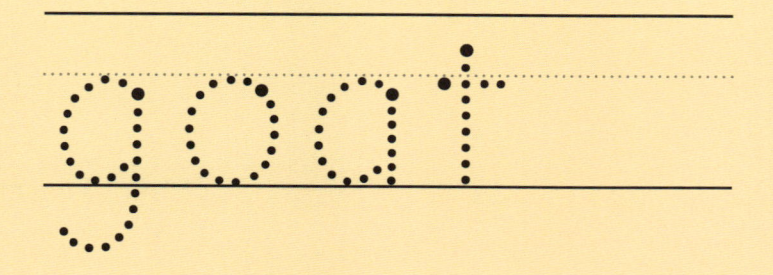

goat

chicken

sheep

dog

tiger

CAN YOU WRITE THE NAMES OF THESE THINGS THAT GO?

plane

truck

tractor

car

rocket

boat

bicycle

train

CAN YOU WRITE SOME WORDS THAT DESCRIBE PEOPLE?

I

you

he

she

we